HUNDRED-YEAR WAVE

Also by Rachel Richardson

Copperhead

HUNDRED-YEAR WAVE

RACHEL RICHARDSON

Carnegie Mellon University Press
Pittsburgh 2016

ACKNOWLEDGMENTS

Many thanks to the editors of the following publications, in which many of these poems, sometimes in different form, first appeared:

Birmingham Poetry Review: "Cathedral"; *Cave Wall:* "Still" and "Queenstown"; *Cellpoems:* "Theory of Desire: The Wrecks" and "Ultrasound"; *The Collagist:* "A Prow, A View" and "Aquarius"; *Connotation Press: An Online Artifact:* "Port"; *Copper Nickel:* "Theory of Desire: The Animal"; *The Georgia Review:* "'Drowning Doesn't Look Like Drowning'"; *The Greensboro Review:* "Seaside"; *Guernica:* "A Brief History of the Whale Fishery"; *Inch:* "Theory of Desire: The *Essex*"; *Literary Imagination:* "Mistranslation of a Fragment by da Vinci"; *Memorious:* "Labyrinth"; *Michigan Quarterly Review:* "Whale Study" and "At the Cutting-In"; *New England Review:* "Anemones" and "Shearwater"; *One* (Jacar Press): "Transmission"; *Radar Poetry:* "I and Thou," "Nature Show, 3 a.m.," and "Of Whales in Paint; in Teeth; in Wood; in Sheet-Iron; in Stone; in Mountains; in Stars"; *The Rumpus:* "Mirror"; *Swarm:* "The Sisters"; *Texas Review:* "Vigil"; *Tinderbox Poetry Review:* "Tide Book"

"Fog, Land's End," "Heartbeat," "In the Week That My Grandmother Stopped Eating," "Shearwater," "Susan Barnard Gardner, b. 1826, New Bedford," and "Ultrasound" received Dorothy Sargent Rosenberg Prizes in 2010, 2011, and 2013. "Heartbeat" was included in *Two Weeks: A Digital Anthology of Contemporary Poetry* (Linebreak, 2011). "Navigator," "Plath's Cakes," and "Whale Study" were included in the anthology *12 Women* (Carnegie Mellon University Press, 2014).

Thanks for the generous gifts of financial support, time, and community to the National Endowment for the Arts for an Individual Artist Fellowship, the University of North Carolina at Chapel Hill for the Kenan Visiting Writer post, and the Sewanee Writers' Conference for a Walter E. Dakin Fellowship in Poetry. Special thanks to the Dorothy Sargent Rosenberg Memorial Fund, and in particular to Mary Rosenberg for her extraordinary generosity and vision.

I could not have written this book without the encouragement and vast archival resources of my family—Gardners to Allens to Forsters to Millers to Jacksons to Richardsons—a long line of women who never threw anything away. And to Captain Edmund Gardner, my great x4 grandfather, most of all, for thinking to keep a journal of all his voyages.

I also owe thanks to Rebecca Morgan Frank, Melissa Range, Megan Snyder-Camp, Nomi Stone, Lyrae Van Clief-Stefanon, Amy Meckler, Andrew Allport, Rachel Nelson, Nina Riggs, Julia Ridley Smith, Dorothy Hans, Shara Lessley, Tess Taylor, Cleopatra Mathis, Linda Gregerson, Ken Fields, Kelly Richardson, Beth Chimera, and Donovan Hohn, for kinship, counsel, and encouragement along the way. The wit and wisdom of my fantastic students in the UNC Imitations class and the resource librarians at the Nantucket Shipwreck and Lifesaving Museum and New Bedford Whaling Museum cannot be overstated. Gerald Costanzo, Cynthia Lamb, Connie Amoroso, and the rest of Carnegie Mellon University Press: thank you for believing in this book.

And of course my deepest gratitude to David, Olivia, and Cecilia, who buoy me daily.

Book design: Connie Amoroso

CONTENTS

∾

∾

∾

for Susan (Gardner) Miller Jackson and Edith Allen Jackson

and for David, by whom I navigate

I called to the other men that the sky was clearing, and then, a moment later, realised that what I had seen was not a rift in the clouds but the white crest of an enormous wave.

—Ernest Shackleton

NAVIGATOR

Let's say I'm Captain Cook, setting sail to drift
until currents push me
into a certain lane, certain highway
with its humpbacked traffic bobbing along.

My young aren't strapped in the back
flinging Cheerios into the crevices like a game of darts
but moored in the house with my patient wife
so I can seek my destiny here—

And I have no destination, not the Friendly Center
or aquarium—I journey only
to find a *usable route.*

I'm stewing the bones a fourth time
to leach any last savor for my
broth—
              not gumming pirate birthday cake
with seafoam-colored frosting, nor
placing my order at the drive-thru
(no, not a Frosty, not a McRib)—

Place-names are still to be scrawled,
new-minted to mark
this passage, its weather and bits of luck.

The usable route's a velvet highway I'll trace
to parchment—a new day, a new world,

not the GPS lady recalculating—

These words held in my mouth,
these words a way to inscribe *we are not lost*
in a vast expanse of lostness.

NATURE SHOW, 3 A.M.

The blue whale's body adjusts to the polar tide
                    and the tropics, each latitude calibrating
her breath. A nursing mother produces
        fifty gallons of milk per day; her calf
grows ten pounds an hour.

        It's purely mathematical, what we've known
                    about her dive: rate per second, depth.
It's a miracle, the narrator says, as we watch her
recede from the boat
        with their camera suctioned to her back—
now we'll get to see—

        and she begins to descend. The narrator
                    goes quiet. First gray,
then black
        overtake the screen.
            I listen to her disappear
as the camera slips off, again, ending
                what we can know of her, that great pulse
        and signal to follow—

A BRIEF HISTORY OF THE WHALE FISHERY

Elbow-deep in the cool white
they flayed into strips, rolling
the winnowing body

as they unraveled her
and the sharks,
smelling their work, circled

and snapped. Unlucky men
hot-stepping the planks.
Lucky men feasting on stars.

Misfits and criminals.
Whittlers, prophets, magicians, boys.
In distress, smothering in fog

or storm, they hoisted mattresses
into the crow's nest
and set them on fire.

Goodbye sleep.
(Melville: *Who are hearsed*
that die on the sea?)

If not the body itself
lit through—
if not the body

they would use
their beds, the brightest thing
to heave—

if not
the body itself
a lighthouse—

the body:
such thin skin
and gold beneath.

MIRROR

All day I'd been photographing boats.
A study in angles: light on water,
shade on water. In a thunderstorm
he asked me. Among fishermen
casting. I could not look and see
his face without the frame
of froth and rain, sudden waves
up against the pier. He was there, yes,
and I spoke the word—
                        I'm trying to say
it's a true story, even the storm, the blurred
photos we snapped later in the tackle shop,
our faces pebbled with rain,
even our feet so easily knocked
out from under us.

CANTICLE IN THE FISH'S BELLY

How to get to it:
    the heart within
the corset
      made of whalebone
and Parisian leaded satin,
          winter weight.

I can barely breathe.

Sun filters from high windows
    into this dark-paneled room

where my sisters help me step
into the skirt,
         our grandmother's grandmother's
sent-for dress, its pinprick satin buttons
down my chest.
    We hook each hook
to hold the corset flush,
        to anchor
the bustle, as she did for her quiet
February wedding,
      snow covering the steeple
of the Seamen's Bethel.

      Melville: *This, shipmates, is that other lesson:*

fasten the locks, hold the heart
within its watery chamber.
        When the seamstress slid
the bone into the bodice
    and pinned each

cut piece together,
                the satin stood upright
at the sewing table.
She could almost
       see it breathe.

I am swallowed
and swallowed whole. It outlasts
          all our vows.

AQUARIUS

But this is about the sea.

      Her body, which envelops.
Which is a living organism
as well as a home.
                      And what about pleasure?
      Love is not a diminished thing:
I love my husband
          even as I would leave him for the sea.

And pleasure, pleasure—   the answer
           why the first humans carved with flint
           the insides out of trees.

To enter the sea,
and be rocked—

To lie in the hollow of one body
afloat inside the next. . . .

This is where I was:

      a body. Lying in the hollow of a tree.

Waiting to be pushed out into the open,
          into the other body, the sea.

QUEENSTOWN

Last port of the Titanic, *1912*

You bring the matching luggage
that doesn't fit on the rack,
the wheels clattering on cobblestones
to get here. You the maker, the carrier.
Pats of butter, barrels of whiskey onboard.

You bring the horse, head braced
against the bracing wind.
The lamplit windows along the shore,
handfuls of weathered lace.
The made, the unmaking.
You the tender, the ferryman
folded in for the night.

A heavy day, heavy tide,
rank with callers of names,
goodbyes. What do you
set for, what unknown?
Instruments boarded, manuscripts,
mink coats and cut glass,
their wedges of light.
You, the messenger through the graveyard.
Singer of bones, singer of bones.

HER STILLNESS

One sailor woke from dreaming, looked overboard: a red flare.
                              Then turned.
The men whispered along her decks, caring
but unconcerned. The wide blackness of night. The whiteness itself
rose like a shore, or a band of steamers, their craggy hulls.

    The night, waiting. Its pearly eye. The *Californian* trembled,
rocked with the undersea tide.
                              If, in the distance, a ship listed, she
did not know it. Her saving was her stillness.
                              If, in the distance, she was wanted,
she slept. Ice surrounded her like a cradle.

THEORY OF DESIRE: THE *ESSEX*

As if a whale had not stove her.
As if she had awaited this dismantling
like a penitent—*the ocean*
was inside her, men later said
of that morning. Meaning how
she went down. The grace. The certainty
that nothing would be retrieved.

MISTRANSLATION OF A FRAGMENT BY DA VINCI

Who'd want to know
what lay beneath those bodies
that created her?

The bed is decaying,
even now, mold

ruining the horsehair
that supported their thrashing.
Understand? Our words

are always trying
to make the darkness

instruct us. Why
do we persist?
Whatever makes a thing

unmakes it too.
If you were a carpenter

would you make boxes
just to learn
to take them apart?

SERPENTINITE, JASPER, AND CLAY

In my ears you were loved, my hallways
and in the bed we slept in, half
submerged below the street
in your cheap apartment
in the chert and shale of Bernal Heights
with its succulents thrusting
from rock terraces and the sky
a cold sponge. In my thighs
and calves you were loved, compacted
like jam jarred on a ledge, crushed
fruits strained and distilled
so thick the light couldn't
come through. Tangerine,
spearmint, black plum.
In my shoulders, in my hands
that scrubbed your face. In my face—
my eyes, my breath.
In the dark, where our faces disappeared
entirely—half pebbles, half sand, a shell
with the shore trapped inside.
In the folded hill, the Pacific Plate subducted
under the North American Plate,
the red and green minerals
smashed against each other
in oxidation, in hill and summit,
in my hard breath against your neck.
In milkweed and trash,
the freeway, the sheet of sun
hanging from the sky.

PLATH'S CAKES

A dough spirals,
                    making itself
from the assembled
ingredients, which
          once together
          cannot be separated.

          (It could be said
there were signs. The sea
howled its hollow song.)

Add heat: a chamber
to bind them.

          (And it could be said
the hawk with the mouse
          not in its talons
          but held in its mouth, alive,
          was the inevitable grasp—)

His pens on her desk,
          muddy shoes
by the door. A stack of white
pages, exacting.

Add heat: a chamber.

          (The bedposts rooted
in the upstairs room—)

Blazing light
          shears from the surf.

Add heat. No wind.

ROGUE WAVE

Everyone thought it was a myth, just
sailors' talk. A story men tell to their wives.

The Captain said, *It came out of the darkness
and looked like the White Cliffs of Dover.*

"DROWNING DOESN'T LOOK LIKE DROWNING"

It looks like dancing the merengue,

like reading *Anna Karenina* on a tablet in the dark car,
the window's greening glow against the night.

Or: like the horse in the stall waiting for the gun
and the gate thumping open.

Maybe the refraction through a shattered bottle,
the way the sun splits it into colors.

It looks like the woman you pretended
not to know at the supermarket
praying among the pickles.

That one. She's singing. Don't tell me
you don't know the words.

EROSION   *[EROS]*

Ocean baits the rock—
calls the layers of schist   *[what fated her]*

to reveal themselves,   *[what she meets]*
split wide.

Like that girl   *[downward years]*
you were, waiting
at the foreign station   *[foamless weirs]*

for a train that wouldn't come
for hours.

Silence
in the blown-out air   *[and fades]*

and even the shuffle of birds   *[pounding wave]*
flapping into the shelter a kind

of silence, impacted.

Ocean baits the rock—   *[as it should be]*
whispers *come,* then licks
straight up the flank.   *[ever could be]*

And you, still a girl
somewhere

in your mind,
still having not boarded,   *[have striven]*

now stand at the cliff edge,
extend your arm   *[changed familiar tree]*

and reach—   *[stairway to the sea]*

                                                             [are driven]

AT THE CUTTING-IN

In the head, the best of it:
oil for lamps, enough
light for every street
in London.
You confuse the meaning
when you say the *soul*,
meat, the *belly*. No,
it is the head
that houses the best.

One must be a carver,
an artist, no green
tinker flaying—

every gleaming ounce
will offer itself
to the man with the jar
and the steady hand.

THEORY OF DESIRE: THE WRECKS

Thousands of ships settle into ocean beds,
tangled reefs and rocks a peopled sea

of rusted steel and old, smooth wood.
Water silks over the wrecks.

It's like they're sleeping, a quiet rhythm
stippling their dark architecture.

HEARTBEAT

You, tenebrous. You're clustered. One cell to another
you meet and divide. Nothing yet here to speak of,
the walls resounding—
                    as when we moved into
the new house: months of rearranging furniture.
And nights in winter, we heard the joints
crack like they would give; by morning
a new seam coursed the paint, a doorframe
had opened its stitching. We busied
ourselves hemming curtains, nailing hooks.
Stacking plates and washing plates and stacking plates.
This is how it happens: patterns.
                            One day
you're breathing. One day all the books are on shelves
and we can pull them down by instinct. Rugs are laid out.
The walls quiet, warmed. It's spring and surprising
shoots present themselves around the oak tree. Meanwhile
you, beating. You quiet, in draft form. You're working.
Oh, we say one morning: daffodils.

ULTRASOUND

Novel unbegun,
half-loaf rising,
lighthouse northward
and anchor south.

Lemon to grapefruit,
you sleep-step sidewise,
turnover, pop-up,
tongue in the mouth.

A GIFT CANNOT BE REFUSED,

                    says the body,
contracting as the infant sucks
at the breast. This is how the uterus returns
to its former size: the baby tells
the body it has finished one task
and embarked on another. Here's the thing,
says the body, I wanted lace and feathers.
Here's the thing, says the body,
not that you asked.

SUSAN BARNARD GARDNER,
B. 1826, NEW BEDFORD

I lived in a small room, my gable facing out
toward the sea. My father lined the sill with scrimshaw
because a sailor never forgets
men bailing the waves, men stove by the beast. . . .

A quarterboard hung from our hearth,
the planks of its ship refixed
as floors and cabinets.
Father quizzed us on each shoal, on maps

of lightships numbered, named.
Told tales of men burning mattresses in rigging:
this is what happens on a foggy night.
This is what happens when the keeper sleeps.

TIDE BOOK

~

let's say the refinery is a beehive
           and the heavy smoke
    wafting
        not smothering—

something is boiling beneath

something stirs
the bleached carapaces strewn
     everywhere
on the sand

limbs   claws   those fragile
     crenellated shells
that small children gather
in their hands—

~

blue crabs sashay
    from their holes;

the big box store sells lottery tickets
as well as lawn chairs

(one can never have too much luck)

∾

I still speak to you
through my skin

half-mother, half-fog

what was the light before dawn? _____

I answered every question
it was milk

∾

we've always kept time
    by the tides

        but also   genealogy

    daughter of daughter of daughter of daughter of daughter of

∼

the station's bell echoes up
    a buoy mid-sleep

the baby never opens her eyes
she knows her way by smell, by sound

       the milk, the sand, seabirds, the moon

       me-you, me-you, me-you

∼

before there was wind there was _____

the baby turns her face
            into the towel

there is too much light

                it gets inside everything, guts it

a song wafts by
            as a girl skirts the residue of froth, tide's shadow

            H is for hyacinth—
            The opposite of roof is reveal—

∼

DOUBLE AQUARIUS

A good sign, my friend says,
to be born under the new moon, the two luminaries conjoined—
a focused sign. And the girl sleeps soundly,
as if she knows it, through rain
and the furnace humming, through the creaks
of our bed, our nightly shuffling traverses
of silvered hallway. Only her hunger
                             wakes her—one grunt
and my nipple throbs. Barred owls hunt in the expanse
of suburban yards as she snuffles and swallows,
sucks and swallows. Yesterday, while she drowsed
                             drunk with milk,
I skimmed articles about human speech evolving from birdsong—
                             Now, in daylight,
chickadees flit in low branches of the crepe myrtle.
She's bundled in the blanket I fold three ways
to contain her. Inside, eyes fluttering again
toward sleep, she cranes her neck
then stills. The owls are long gone with their rabbits;
last night's kitchen mouse scratches in its trap.
                             In their paper on human language structure,
the researchers found a series of complex
patterns—the Bengalese finch,
for example, loops back to previous melodies
to expand its message; the nightingale
may sing us two hundred different songs.
                             (Not to us—*to who? to who?*)
Twisted and restrung, sung and sung—
the noonlit yard appears dead, its brown-gray grass
stiff from another night's freeze. But the buds
cling to every branch, hard,

waiting to blossom. They make a sound
when they finally appear—
crying? singing? a rhythmic hum?
Whatever they say, the bees hear them, and come.

CONSTELLATION

I'm passing the age now,
that year you lost the girls

when the car drove itself
into the tree. Fifty-eight springs later

the bark hasn't absorbed
the scar. It must have seemed

sheer will: the movement of the wheel
under your hands,

the desire of the machine
for the crash. While you slept,

that second, two, three,
your girls were held in the arms

of steel, that boat
of a car, advertised all over the *Globe*

for innovation and quiet, a purr
rather than a roar.

I'm passing you, as I must, as you would
tell me I must:

a woman frozen in the steaming
hulk, the steering wheel locked

against your crumpled chest.
I can't stop to retrieve you,

nor pull those small bodies
from the wreck, where they lay

stranded between this world
and the next,

and the shattered glass around them
glinted at nothing

in the gathering dark.

A PROW, A VIEW

(Susan Miller Jackson, 1918-2010)

There's video now
of anything you desire: a prow, a view
of the ragged coast receding, ropes wound

around the cleat, smooth curve of sanded planks
along a sun-warmed deck.

Names catch in the crevices
on the way to your brain—
but your eyes, yellowed and milky, still

focus on the bow and the compass; your hands
still reach for the wheel.

Here's the spouting of a pod,
here's a breach, here the fish that follow
in a wake of blood.

Every morning I bring you my offerings—
little treasures from the morning surf.

We watch the sailors, the whales,
the endless waves, until you look up
from your hospital cot,

surveying the sky for fair winds,
preparing your voyage.

WHALE STUDY

They go down.
The distance beyond light
only tells their route by the scars
they bear back to the surface.
In such depths night opens,
breathes, unsplit by rays
of sun. A quiet snow falls;
hatchetfish lower their jaws.
So many nights I have wept
for the city of my childhood,
imagining it sunk—but for them
there is no floor,
here past the shore-hugging tides,
wrecks glittering with rust
still oozing rainbows upward—

they go down hunters, blind.
Memory is a map. Midnight
presses deep against
their mammalian hide.

CATHEDRAL

On a snowy rise
bright with silence,
the wet, heavy branches
of pines newly clothed in snow
and no tracks yet
from animal or vehicle,
with that cottony closeness
of the frigid air
undisturbed, that
palace made of lace,
of ice, and nothing
and no one
and no road remaining
but the path between trees
to wend the way
deeper into quiet
and the whiteness
complete, blinding
                    —I corkscrewed,
spun, came to rest
in a drift.

Sat watching
the weightless flakes
drop from the burdened trees.
Praised nothing.

BOY IN BLUEBIRD PAJAMAS

They're dead, they're dead, they're dead!,
he trills, delight welling up that a sound
could be a hammer, could open
and close across his palate in the single
syllable.

You still have four, a neighbor says,
kindly, three years later, patting
my grandmother's arm.

Some nights, when he's older, he steals
up to the third floor and crawls
across the wood, patting the bedspreads
of his sisters with his outstretched hand.

She spreads jam on brown sliced bread
arranged like tiles down the length
of the counter. She still has four.
She watches them, here
at the window. The rope swing they've
abandoned makes a slow ellipse
in the yard.

THE UNMAKING

after snow artist Simon Beck

Having walked
    the frozen lakes
        for hours,

his prints circle
    and circle,
each expansion a rendering
of new pattern—

the artist
    obscuring himself
in the
    interlocking
spheres of white
        (for what is better
    erasure than snow?).

And when
the lake warms, or
        the snow blows
across the field
with a sudden wind,

    the tracks that stroked
this freeze all day
vanish.

The unmaking
smooth,
      like a tablecloth
    swept from a table.

It's why I love it.
It's why
        I never go there
anymore.

LABYRINTH

At the entrance of the cave
I watch my sister's flippers kick into black; I breathe
my steady long breath into the respirator.

Overhead, the shadow
of a boat covers us, then releases us into the rays
of watery sun.

In the myth
there are always two sisters: one who enters,
one who waits.

I circle
so as not to lose this passage
among the coral mounds, the undersea castles.

I'm her monkfish
mothering, half-blind in the mask
that shows me only the tiny details of the closest creatures.
For example, the bitten fin of this hammerhead. Not the faraway figure
emerging.

Nothing but darkness here at the mouth.
And the wavering flit of two clownfish as they dart, together
then apart, into a cluster of anemones.

NOTES ON "NATURE SHOW, 3 A.M."

Suddenly, blue. The windows gloss as the whale
                        descends. This television's glow is drowning
            the room.

            (In the London record of deaths
            in 1665, fall, this is given
        as cause for one: *Suddenly.*
            Amid *stillbirth* and *dropsie* and *plague.*)

Upstairs my humans sleep,
                        and cradled next to me like an animal
            the pump wheezes its greedy wheeze.

Narrator: *A nursing calf grows ten pounds an hour.*

        Dear enormous children
with your candlesticks at the bedside,
                here are fifty gallons of milk.

        (To the cannibal rats on the ghost ship,
                    even meat and fur began to taste
            like milk.)

                        (In the London record, one died
                        starved at Nurse.)

Narrator: *She's gone . . . she's gone. . . .*

        Here's my seabed tune,
metronome to each cream ounce:

Dear blueness/blackness, inverse light,
dear skin and milk beneath.
Da-*dum*, da-*dum*, da-*dum*, da-*dum*.
One died frighted. One died of grief.

THE SISTERS

My sister the contortionist
sleeps naked on a wire,
and my sister the planner
sleeps cradled against her phone,
its muffled buzz like an infant's
quick shudder, or a tiny dog's.
My sister the thief sleeps with a knife
between the sheets, and
my sister the president
sleeps in a chair she's fitted
with magnets and ergonomic bolsters.
My sisters the twins wait
for me to climb into my own bed
before slipping out the window
to their treehouse mats.
My sister the Iditarod racer
sleeps in the snow, and in summer
climbs into the deep freeze,
packing herself in buffalo meat.
My sister the antelope
is displeased with our ruckus
—wants to know why
we need such accommodation
when she sleeps in a pile
of laundry or the thick grass
at the back of the yard.
One of us is always howling.
One of us is waiting to be called.
Tell her she has sisters,
though she will not need to be told.

ASTRONOMER

A child climbs into a cardboard house,
shuts its door and windows
to hold in the dark, and lies on her back
inside, looking up through its cut-out moon
and stars. She knows she is not looking
at the sky. But she calls out, still,
It's nighttime! I'm looking at the sky!

THEORY OF DESIRE: THE ANIMAL

The lobster doesn't like it
when we eat him, my daughter posits—
a point I knew was coming
after naming *chicken* in the neighbor's coop and *chicken*
on her plate. *Animals eat other animals,* I shrug.
This is hours after I've read
that Captain Pollard's crew, 74 days adrift, drew lots
to choose who would sustain the others
with his meat.

I want a claw, she says, reaching.
Behind the breathy traffic
on Water Street, we hear a shout
rise from the bar, a staticky cheer
that resettles as the crowd resumes drinking
and another player on the wide screen
saunters up to bat. *The animal that gets eaten*
never likes it, I say, though
I read many men, perhaps even
Pollard himself, lay down in the bottom
of the whaleboat, covered themselves
in salt-crusted canvas, and prayed.

I like my lot
as well as any other, said Owen Coffin
before his childhood playmate took up the gun.

Inside the claw, the sweet flesh.
Inside the bones,
even of a starved man, the marrow.
The blue whale's skeleton, displayed

in New Bedford since 1998,
still oozes rich oil onto the museum's wood floors.
It is fragrant and golden in hue.

IN THE WEEK THAT MY GRANDMOTHER STOPPED EATING

                        Her daughter's lover
mapped trees for sugaring. Cows lowed
over the hill. The sweet smell of dung
carried in on the pads of kittens
who curled near her feet by the stove.
                                 From what I hear
they lay plate after plate before her and each time,
to each petitioner, she turned up her open face
and smiled at them, whoever they were—
                                    everyone by now
her kin, everyone her child, alternately begging
and forcing the bread against her teeth.

She said nothing, until she said thank you,
and then turned back to the window, which she had no need
to see beyond.

VIGIL

There's nothing left to do about the bees
that cloak the table and sofa, dazed in
the work of occupying the
dusky space, its vessels. As the stomach
aches for its milk. Swarm. Not sweat
of labor, nor voices calling a hum across
a calm tableau. *You, come here to me*, the
weary woman used to say. Creased brow.
Worn hands. Bees mass in her armchair. *Come now.*

STILL

He'd lost two girls already, so to see this bed
a rack of flame, to watch it bloom

like weeds conquering the frame, was to believe
another daughter curled inside, feeding the fire.

He called to her, my mother, before he hoisted it.
Her name: *Edie*—and when she emerged

from the vacant room, he knew
she was safe. Still, it was four a.m., winter,

his daughter's nest of blankets afire, billowing
around the idea of her body. Her still body.

He lifted that mattress somehow, shoved it
out the window. At dawn, the younger children woke

to the tamped smoke and watched their father
on the gable in the snow, stamping the embers,

beating the mattress apart. Soot lifted into air;
the rest was laid wet into the earth.

FOG, LAND'S END

Love for   the particle,   particulate,
for   the whiteness,   yes,   enveloping,
and   for the   rickety   steps
where I   climbed   with my   good red   dog,
the dirt   clumped,   kicked up
along   the wood   ladder   to another   plateau
of trail.   For vision   kaleidoscoped,
for pie   chart,   love for   the bridge
just   poking   its orange   prow   from cloud.
Pieces   of   sea.   Nothing   to   be taken in
full-mouthed,   nothing   lacquered
but   particulate,   held   in the   hand,   this air
like bread   I inhale   wetly,   the animal's
breath   steaming.   Lift me,   break
me   down.   Stroke me   with your   million   pearls.

TRANSMISSION

There was a girl who heard it happen:
Amelia Earhart calling
on the radio, she and her navigator
alternately cursing and defining their position
by latitude, as best they could read it
in the bellowing wind, and by what
they could surmise of their rate per hour,
last land they'd seen. *Stay with me, someone,*
and the girl wrote each word
in her composition book, kept the channel
tuned, hunched to the receiver
when static overtook the line.
Why do I think of her?
The coast guard laughed at her father
holding out the schoolgirl scrawl
and sent him home ashamed. A lost woman
is a lost woman, he told her, and the sea
is dark and wide.

PORT

Sing, mockingbird,
if you're the one left to me,
your sultry pidgin
of east and west.
What have I ever asked for
but a word that began
and ended in the same place?
I admit my mongrel tongue.
I'll take the *non sono qui,*
your morning quip.
The lemons are so ripe they thud
and spring the branch.
Who am I to speak?
Let me hear the song,
however patched.
A rhyme still traces
the shadow of skyline
though ruins are what's left
of the city itself.

I AND THOU

Some nights I can't even bear
to reach for you. Your long,
long legs, the birthmark
that blooms across
one shoulder, your mineral-blue
eyes turning and turning
over the broken-down relics
my family hoards.
You, of unknown origin:
chimney sweeps
and cemetery crews.
Builders of road
my people clattered down,
unthinking. What is marriage
but two ships passing,
one sending its captain
aboard the other for a gam?
No. That's me hijacking
the metaphor again. My people
are of water, yours of stone.
Yet the Nantucket Quakers
believed in hailing their fellows
as *thou*—a warmth, a bridge
from *you* to *me*.
As in this wave-soaked sand.
The point of erosion.
Our bodies, lying here,
make the seam.

SEASIDE

Summer is a day. The terns swirl
on the wind, letting it toss them
this way and that, then
dive—their bodies arrow
into the shallow waves.

~

A pair of urns on the mantel
twined with a Japanese floral pattern,
a delicate pink petal—

~

Each day I listen through closed eyes
to the waves lick the beach,
the sun kaleidoscoping bright shapes
inside my lids. One daughter fills a bucket
with periwinkles, then
empties it into the surf.
One daughter kicks on a towel in the shade
of an enormous umbrella,
dazzled at the movement of the air.

My grandmother came here
fifty-two more summers
after her daughters died. Even now
in the leaning garage
stand their small bicycles.

~

This wind. These pressed flowers
falling out of the old hardbound
Robinson Crusoe, Just So Stories—
their weightless drift to table.

~

This day. This hour. The mossy shingles
by the outdoor shower. Summer is a day.

~

In my grandmother's last year,
my mother asked me to wipe
as she held the frail woman
above the toilet bowl. Her body had reduced
to sinew, slack. Her cotton pants billowed
around her knees. In a thousand wisps
around her face, her long hair fell,
too fine to be held in the braids the children
still each morning wound around her head.
I had never been asked to minister.
I had hardly touched her in years.

ANEMONES

Earliest memory: leaves of the olive tree
fluttering, the light coming through,
then not, then through, then not—

My horoscope advises me to avail myself
of the mystery
            —and though I've never been a believer,
though I tie my shoes to the leg of the bed
in case of fire or quake because I *won't*
give myself to such flame
            —still I can't help
watching these anemones
here in the tidepool, swayed by water's
whim, waving their many tentacles,
no direction, no intention—

OF WHALES IN PAINT; IN TEETH; IN WOOD; IN SHEET-IRON; IN STONE; IN MOUNTAINS; IN STARS

I

Desire, if ever found,
        if ever hauled up with a deep hook
and stripped

        of its algae and rust
and sanded down
        and burnished to its new
seawashed sheen
                (a smoothness, an interiority
                exposed)

might save. That lucky ship
        is years gone from the harbor,
no word delivered home
        though the crew
            surely wrote at every port.

Turning away from you
            and you from me
        in our bed, falling into shared

silence in a curtained room
        is perhaps like this,
or perhaps
        nothing like this.

II

Some men carved
                their wives' faces
        into the whales' teeth
they saved
        from the try-pots—

in their bunks
                (their lamps lit
        with spermaceti) they caressed
the horned pearl
        or in fair weather worked
on deck. The slip
                of a finger might make her
a mermaid, leg-line
        curling into a tail—
or give her a child
                clinging to the hem
        of her woolen dress.

III

And looking up at a sky
        without a city
to blunt it

                (I never said
        I was lonely)

is a wonder:
the cetacean world
        cavorts in the heavens.

How to explain the depth

        (I never said it but perhaps
                it still was true)

—the depth of such desire
                not to have a body

at all, but be
        phosphorescent?

                In other words
        be the flame

not pilot light.
        Be fire in service
of itself.

SHEARWATER

You were given feet but had never touched
them to earth. You were given the sea
and you fed upon it for months.

So when your head crowned, ashen
with loss of blood from the cord
wound tight around your neck,

and when they cut you from me,
and you were silent, and the tide in me
receded, I remembered the shearwaters

following the ship—the slow sweep
of them riding the wind's current.
The stretch of them, hovering,

cruciform, shearing the air the way an envelope
slides back into a box of letters, making
its narrow space. I had watched

from the stern for hours their trailing:
as if stillness itself drifted toward me.
I thought it was my life.

Then someone lifted you up,
and there was a sound,
and they laid you on me, breathing.

NOTES

"Canticle in the Fish's Belly" takes its title and italicized line from Herman Melville's *Moby-Dick*. The term is used by Father Mapple, in his sermon in the Seamen's Bethel in New Bedford, as he discusses Jonah's redemption from within the belly of the whale.

In "Her Stillness," the *Californian* was a British steamship in close range of the *Titanic* on the night she sank. There was wireless radio communication between the two vessels, and the *Californian* could see the *Titanic's* distress rockets, but she did not offer aid.

"Theory of Desire: The *Essex*" refers to the whaleship stove by a sperm whale in 1820—a source of inspiration for Melville in writing *Moby-Dick*.

"Rogue wave" is a term used to describe the rare ocean phenomenon in which a surprisingly large wave forms, inconsistent with the sea state around it. These waves are also called freak, monster, killer, and abnormal waves. The Draupner wave was measured on January 1, 1995, in the North Sea, and confirmed the existence of rogue waves, which had until then been thought possibly mythical. The quote in the poem comes from newspaper accounts of the RMS *Queen Elizabeth II* during Hurricane Luis in 1995.

"Serpentinite, Jasper, and Clay" owes a debt to Shara Lessley for some of its language, and is for David Roderick.

"Erosion   [*Eros*]": The italicized text at the right of the poem is fragments taken from Edwin Arlington Robinson's "Eros Turannos."

"Susan Barnard Gardner, b. 1826, New Bedford" was informed and aided by *Captain Edmund Gardner of Nantucket and New Bedford: His Journal and His Family*, Ed. John M. Bullard (The Cabinet Press, 1958).

"Double Aquarius" is for Cleopatra Mathis.

"Theory of Desire: The Animal": In the aftermath of the *Essex* sinking, its twenty-man crew floated in three whaleboats for months. In Captain George Pollard's boat, after food and water had run out, the men voted to draw lots to determine who should be sacrificed for the survival of the others. Owen

Coffin, Pollard's cousin and the youngest member of the crew at age 17, drew the black spot. His boyhood friend, Charles Ramsdell, then drew the lot that made him Coffin's executioner. The Pollard boat was eventually sighted, 95 days after the sinking, off the coast of South America by another Nantucket whaleship, the *Dauphin*. In the end, eight crewmembers were rescued from the two boats that were found, seven more having been eaten. The final boat with its five crewmembers was never found. Nathaniel Philbrick's *In the Heart of the Sea* (Viking, 2000) is the book I mention in the poem. I also consulted the New Bedford Whaling Museum and Research Library, and Owen Chase's *Narrative of the Most Extraordinary and Distressing Shipwreck of the Whale-Ship Essex* (1821).

"Vigil" pays homage to Gwendolyn Brooks by borrowing a line of hers to use as end-words for the new poem. My line, "Bees in the stomach, sweat across the brow. Now." comes from Brooks's "Appendix to the Anniad."

"Transmission" is based on the story of Betty Klenck Brown, a 15-year-old in St. Petersburg, Florida, at the time of Amelia Earhart's World Flight. She was likely the last person to have heard Earhart's voice.

"Seaside": The line "Summer is a day" is from Kenneth Fields's poem "Watermelon in Easter Hay," borrowed with permission.

"Of Whales in Paint; in Teeth; in Wood; in Sheet-Iron; in Stone; in Mountains; in Stars" borrows its title from the title of chapter 57 in *Moby-Dick*.